ABCs
for
Life

26 Principles for
Success and Happiness

JAMES R. BALL

KEEP IT SIMPLE FOR SUCCESS™

ABCs for Life
26 Principles for Success and Happiness

ISBN: 1-887570-03-9

Published in the United States by The Goals Institute. Printed in the United States.

Keep It Simple for Success™ is a registered trademark of The Goals Institute.

For information please contact or visit us at:

The Goals Institute
P.O. Box 3736
Reston, VA 20195-1736

www.goalsinstitute.com
www.kissbooks.com
Email: info@goalsinstitute.com

*Dedicated to
Jennifer and Stephanie,
the music in my life*

Welcome

HELLO!

My name is Jim Ball, and I want to welcome you on behalf of all of us at The Goals Institute and our *Keep It Simple for Success*™ team.

What you have in your hands is a concise summary of what we call the *ABCs for Life: 26 Principles for Success and Happiness*.

Congratulations for having this book. It is an A-to-Z reference and guide to help you achieve what you want to achieve, become what you want to become, and do what you want to do—both in your career and in your personal life.

No one can guarantee success or happiness, however, I believe that these 26 principles are essential and that you will increase your odds for success and happiness if you will just read and follow them.

If you have any questions or comments, please drop us a note or send us an email.

If you would like additional information about our other *Keep It Simple for Success*™ books or our keynotes and seminars, please visit us at our website at www.kissbooks.com.

Best wishes for great joy,

Contents

A

Attitude

ATTITUDE is your window on the world.

Your attitude is the perspective through which you see, interpret, and respond to the world, and the world looks back, interprets, and responds to you.

If you have a positive and optimistic attitude you will see the world full of possibilities and opportunities, and you will see people as friendly and helpful.

With a negative and pessimistic attitude, however, you will see the world full of obstacles and problems, and you will see people as unfriendly roadblocks.

It all starts with you and your attitude.

Do:

- Think, talk, and act positively.
- Focus on the possibilities.
- Surround yourself with positive people.
- Work in a positive, nurturing environment.

Don't:

- Think, talk, or act negatively.
- Dwell on obstacles and problems.
- Associate with negative people.
- Work in a negative, depressing environment.

Belief

BELIEF is your ability to see with confidence and without doubt things as realized before they are realized.

Your beliefs govern the heights and limitations of what you will and will not pursue, accomplish, and become.

If you really believe one hundred percent that you can accomplish something, then you will act confidently and boldly. This will attract people and resources to you and increase your odds for success.

If you do not believe that you can accomplish something or have doubt, then you will hesitate and act with reservation. This will drive people and resources from you and increase your odds for failure.

You can change your beliefs by changing your self-talk, the images you hold, and the actions you take.

Do:

- Use self-talk, such as *I can* and *I am*.
- Visualize images of what you want to believe.
- Act as though it is already so.

Don't:

- Use self-talk, such as *I cannot* or *I am not*.
- Hold images of what you do not want to believe.

Choice

CHOICE is your miracle of creation.

Choice is the power that you have to determine what you will or will not become, accomplish, and experience in life. You exercise your power of choice by selecting what you think, value, desire, and do.

You seal your fate with the big and little choices you make: Big choices like where to live, whom to marry, and what career to pursue. Little choices like what to eat, when to exercise, and whether to smile or to frown. Like compound interest, your choices will accumulate over time, and they will create you and your life.

Do:

- Use your power of choice to decide what you want to do, accomplish, and become.
- Choose what you really want, and choose big.
- Pay attention to the little choices in life, too.

Don't:

- Let life just take you without taking time to think through your alternatives and make choices.
- Let others choose for you.
- Underestimate the cumulative lifetime effect of all the little choices you make.

D

Desire

DESIRE is the engine that creates your power.

Your desire determines the heat and intensity of all your pursuits.

If you have a white-hot burning desire, you will summon the greatest of your powers and strengths, and you will be able to face and overcome any obstacles, tasks, or challenges that may come your way.

If you have only a small desire, one that has no flame, then you will not be able to create or sustain enough power to achieve or attain what you really want.

Do:

- Get excited!
- Pursue your dreams with all the passion that you can possibly muster.
- Pursue only those goals that you strongly desire.
- Fuel your desire by increasing your exposures.

Don't:

- Ignore your desires.
- Waste time pursuing goals you do not care about.

E

Enthusiasm

ENTHUSIASM is the fuel to your energy.

Your enthusiasm is the sister to your desire. It creates and maintains the excitement and momentum you need to begin the pursuit of major goals and to overcome obstacles you may encounter.

Nothing great or brilliant was ever achieved without enthusiasm. Without enthusiasm, no game was ever won and no success was ever achieved.

To ignite your enthusiasm, do what you love and believe in and do it with passion. To be enthusiastic, act enthusiastically, talk enthusiastically, and think enthusiastically.

Do:

- Pursue your passions.
- Think enthusiastically.
- Talk enthusiastically.
- Act enthusiastically.

Don't:

- Let others dampen your enthusiasm or spirits.
- Think, talk, or act in a downtrodden manner.

Focus

FOCUS is the key to your effectiveness.

When you focus, you prioritize your choices, eliminate alternatives not to be pursued, and concentrate your full attention, resources, and energies on a narrow selection of goals and courses of action.

Most people do not achieve their full potential because they diffuse their efforts by pursuing too many alternatives. Rather than selecting one or two major tasks or goals to pursue, they spend their time throughout the day, week, and month in drabs and dribbles doing a little bit of everything.

It is better to pursue one thing and do it well than to pursue multiple alternatives with mediocre results.

Do:

- Pursue only one or two major goals at a time.
- Prioritize your alternatives and select those that are the most important.
- Eliminate low priority alternatives.

Don't:

- Diffuse your efforts on too many initiatives.
- Get distracted once you set a course of action.

Goals

GOALS are tools that you use to create your life.

Goals enable you to become what you want to become and accomplish what you want to accomplish.

Goals are not just end results to be achieved; goals are the stepping stones to the life that you will live.

You are already on a path based upon goal choices you have already made. Take the time now to look down that path and evaluate if it is headed where you want to end up. If not, you can change your path and final destination by simply changing your goals.

When you select a goal, make sure that you are very clear and exact about what you want to achieve.

Do:

- Take time to decide the goals you want to pursue.
- Select goals that will make you into the person you want to become and will cause you to achieve the results you want to achieve.

Don't:

- Let others direct your life by dictating the goals you will pursue.

Habits

HABITS are your guidance system.

Your habits will determine what you become and accomplish. All of your habits, good and bad, are the tracks that your train of life runs upon.

We literally *are* what we repeatedly do and we *do* what we repeatedly think about.

Depending on where you want to go, you must adopt thinking and acting habits that will take you there. If your existing habits are taking you where you don't want to go, then you need to replace them.

Do:

- Take an inventory of your habits and decide which ones you want to keep, which ones you want to eliminate, and which new ones you want to acquire.
- Create routines, rituals, and processes that will help you acquire the habits you desire.

Don't:

- Underestimate the importance of your habits.
- Ignore bad habits that are driving you down paths toward results that you do not want.

Individuality

INDIVIDUALITY is the gift that you were given for yourself and that you give to others.

There never was or ever will be another person exactly like you. You are an original, one-of-a-kind miracle.

To preserve your uniqueness, rather than trying to be like everyone else, you must continually strive to understand and express your own individuality. Because there are pressures from every corner to conform, this is not easy. Easy or not, you must try.

Whatever you are, you are all you have. And what you have is sufficient if you will only discover it and use it to light your life.

Do:

- Find some quiet time to ponder who you are, what you desire, and what unique abilities you have.
- Express yourself and your individuality.

Don't:

- Conform to the ways and desires of the crowd if to do so means that you must sacrifice important aspects of your individuality.
- Be afraid to be yourself.

Joy

JOY is the music in your life.

Your joy is your happiness, laughter, and bliss. When you are joyful, your song of life is in perfect harmony.

The peaks of our joy make the valleys of our sadness and sorrow bearable. And while, like with the yin and the yang, there will be difficulties in a complete life, we always can focus on our joyful moments.

Joy is a choice. You can choose to be joyful and happy or you can choose to be sorrowful and sad.

Do:

- Choose to be joyful and happy.
- Enjoy your joyful moments.
- Bring joy into the lives of others.

Don't:

- Choose to be sorrowful and sad.
- Cause sadness or unhappiness for others.

Knowledge

KNOWLEDGE is the source of your alternatives.

Your knowledge is the sum total of what you know and understand.

If you want to be more knowledgeable and have more alternatives, you must become a lifetime reader and learner. You also can increase your knowledge and alternatives by expanding your experiences. Widen the activities you participate in, the variety of people you associate with, and the places you see and experience.

Do:

* Increase your knowledge and alternatives.
* Read all that you can.
* Become a continuous life-long learner.
* es and associations.

what you know.

Your Guide for Life

Use the *ABCs for Life* as your constant guide and companion. Just turn to any page in the book for an instant recharge. Try looking up your initials, your name, or a word that is unique to you to read more about the special guidance those letters provide for you.

To reorder this Pocket Pal™: 1-800-964-6257
www.kissbooks.com
©2002 The Goals Institute

ABCs for Life

Love

LOVE is the ultimate expression of your being.

Love is the greatest force on earth. When you have love in your life, you have true and divine power in your life. When you live with love in your heart, your spirit is invincible to the negativity and obstacles of the world. When you express your love to the world, you are living your life to the fullest.

Whatever you do or pursue in life, do it for love. Marry for love. Serve those whom you love. Be with those whom you love. Do what you love to do.

Do:

- Put love into your life.
- Greet everyone with love in your heart.
- Love one another.

Don't:

- Miss love.
- Put off love.

Manners

MANNERS express your respect for and honor of others.

Your manners are your outward expression of the inner respect and honor that you have for others. Your manners also express your kindness and civility toward them.

When you respect and honor others, they will respect and honor you. When you disrespect others, they will disrespect you.

Two of the most important ways to show your respect are to say *please* and *thank you*. When you ask someone for something, say *please*. When someone gives you a gift, a service, or a kindness, say *thank you*. You can never say please or thank you too often.

Manners matter.

Do:

- Say *please* and *thank you*.
- Be courteous and polite.
- Wait your turn.

Don't:

- Forget to say *please* and *thank you*.
- Push in front of others.

Negativity

NEGATIVITY is a poison that can and will kill you.

When you are negative you cast doubt and despair; snatch dreams away; are undesirable, depressing, and stressful to be around; limit your growth and potential and the growth and potential of others; demotivate and deflate enthusiasm; and destroy your joy and happiness and the joy and happiness of others.

Nothing good comes from being negative. Nothing.

Do:

- Eliminate negativity from your life.
- Adopt a positive outlook.
- Avoid negative people as much as you can.

Don't:

- Be negative.
- Associate with negative people any more than you absolutely have to.

Obstacles

OBSTACLES are challenges that make you strong.

Every obstacle you encounter is an opportunity for you to learn and grow. By addressing your obstacles head-on you will learn and grow from the experiences whether you overcome the obstacles or not.

Most obstacles in life seem bigger than they actually are. They shrink quickly into their small realities when you face them.

Do:

- Address your obstacles head-on.
- Welcome obstacles as opportunities to learn and grow.

Don't:

- Delay or procrastinate when you encounter obstacles.
- Exaggerate obstacles in your mind.

P

Persistence

PERSISTENCE is the transformation of your commitment and determination into action.

There can be no great accomplishments in life without persistence.

Once you decide what you want and make up your mind to realize it, then pursue it one hundred percent and never give up.

Do not let anything or anybody stand in your way. Do not let any obstacle or circumstance deter you. Press on until you achieve what you set out to achieve. Keep on going until you arrive at your destination.

Do:

- Persist, even in the face of obstacles and setbacks.
- Press on.

Don't:

- Quit.
- Think about quitting.
- Say you are going to quit.

Quality

QUALITY is the degree of your pursuit of excellence.

Never accept a mediocre effort or result from yourself. Always push for the best you can be and do. Always try to do it right the first time.

Take pride in your work. Strive for the best in all that you do and you will be thought of in the highest regard. Good quality always shows. Mediocre or poor quality also always shows.

Good enough never is.

Do:

- Pursue excellence in all that you do.
- Be the best you can be, and do the best you can do.

Don't:

- Tolerate mediocrity.
- Cut corners.

Resilience

RESILIENCE is your ability to spring back and recover from setbacks and disappointments.

If you are going to have a successful and happy life, you must learn to be resilient.

Life contains obstacles and disappointments, and you will have your share. At times, it may seem that the obstacles you are encountering are overwhelming. Your setbacks and disappointments may be great.

It is during these dark moments that you must pick yourself up, brush yourself off, suck in your gut, stick out your chest, and move forward, once again, with renewed energy and enthusiasm.

You must rejuvenate yourself when setbacks occur.

Do:

- Spring back after setbacks.
- Adopt a resiliency habit.
- Focus on the future and its opportunities.

Don't:

- Dwell on problems, disappointments, and setbacks.

Simplicity

SIMPLICITY is your mastery of understanding.

The best things in life are usually very simple ideas or concepts executed exceedingly well. Details may be required to produce results, but the best ideas and designs are simple and plain.

Keep things simple and it will be easier to stay on track and be successful.

Speak and write using simple words and plain language. Make your goals and plans simple and clear. Clean out clutter.

Simple is better.

Do:

* Keep things simple.
* Eliminate clutter.
* Streamline.
* Use simple language.

Don't:

* Complicate things.
* Use more steps than necessary.
* Use unnecessary adornments.
* Use big or fancy words.

Time

TIME is your life.

Time is all you have. The time you spend is your life. It is not sand that you see going through the hourglass, it is you. To waste time is to waste your life.

In reality, we cannot manage time. Time just is. What we *can* manage is how we use ourselves while time passes. We can decide how to spend ourselves.

To manage your life, proactively decide what you will spend your time on.

Spend as much of your time as you can in one-hour uninterrupted chunks. This simple technique can make your personal effectiveness zoom.

Do:

- Decide how you will spend your life.
- Spend your time wisely.
- Spend your time in one-hour uninterrupted chunks.
- Make every minute and hour of every day count.

Don't:

- Waste time on activities you do not value.
- Think of time as an infinite resource, for it is not.

U

Up

UP is the direction you should always look and think.

Look up. Raise your sights to goals and plans beyond those that you may have currently.

Think up. Raise your ideals to dreams and achievements that stretch your limits.

Be up in spirit.

Do:

- Look up.
- Think up.

Don't:

- Look down.
- Think down.

Values

VALUES are the foundation stones of your character and reputation.

Your values support and determine all of your thoughts and actions.

If you have good values, you will have good character, and others will treat you accordingly. If you have questionable or bad values, you will have questionable or bad character, and others will treat you accordingly.

Good values include honesty, truthfulness, forthrightness, loyalty, and fairness.

Bad values include dishonesty, lying, cheating, deception, stealing, disloyalty, and unfairness.

Do:

• Adopt good values you are proud to have.
• Protect your reputation by acting only in accordance with good values.

Don't:

• Adopt bad and undesirable values.
• Endanger your reputation; it is the only one you will ever have.

Willpower

WILLPOWER is your inner strength that you can call on to do what you must do when you must do it.

By sheer will, you have the power to begin any pursuit and complete any task. To access your willpower you must summon it through your thoughts, your words, and your actions.

To invoke your willpower, resolve that you will succeed; speak firmly using the words *I will* or *I am*, and act deliberately and willfully.

Think of your willpower as a switch deep within your spirit that you mentally click into the *on* position each time you must get going or keep going.

Do:

- Summon your inner strength.
- Click your willpower into the on position.
- Think, speak, and act willfully.

Don't:

- Think or say *I can't*.

X-factor

X-FACTOR represents the little extras that you do to distinguish your work and results.

It is the extra effort you make to do your work properly. It is the extra touch you add.

It is the extra time you take to learn something new or to teach something new to someone else.

It is the extra few minutes you spend to complete a task for the day.

It is the extra praise, thanks, and appreciation that you express to others.

Do:

* Take the extra step and go the extra mile.
* Pay attention to the details.
* Do more than others expect you to do.
* Add something extra.

Don't:

* Settle for the plain and ordinary.
* Skip the little details.

You

YOU are the most important person in your life.

Whatever you will become and accomplish is up to you and no one else to achieve.

While others may encourage you, assist you in your tasks, and help you pursue your dreams and achieve your goals, you and you alone are responsible for what you do or do not do. You and you alone can bring about the successes you desire. You and you alone can create a life of happiness.

You are the miracle in your life and the power in your life. Your life is in your hands.

Do:

- Trust in yourself.
- Believe in yourself.
- Be accountable to yourself.
- Act and take control of your life.
- Live your life to the fullest.

Don't:

- Rely on others to achieve your dreams for you.
- Wait for others to push you.

Zeal

ZEAL is the fullness and zest in your life.

Your zeal represents the special zing that you bring to life and everyday events.

Put spice into your life by doing ordinary things in extraordinary ways. Read materials that expand your mind. Visit exotic and fantastic places that revitalize your senses. Associate with colorful and fascinating people who make you think and who teach you new things. Surround yourself with fun and lively objects that provoke your creativity.

Do:

* Put zest in your life.
* Try something new and different.
* Experiment and have fun.

Don't:

* Be boring and mundane.
* Be afraid to experiment.

Good, Better, Best

To read is
good.

To read
and think about
what you read is
better.

To read,
think about what you read,
and then act is
best.

—Jim Ball

Here I am, day . . .

The most important progress to make
is daily progress.

Don't wake up in the morning
and say here I am, day,
take me!

The day surely will take you,
if you let it.

Wake up instead and say,
here I am, day, and this is what I am
going to do and accomplish!

Then do it.

—Jim Ball

About the Author

JAMES R. BALL is CEO of The Goals Institute, a company that helps businesses and organizations achieve their potential through goal achievement.

Through The Goals Institute, Mr. Ball provides executive development programs and keynote speeches for corporations and organizations. He also is a co-creator of the *Keep It Simple for Success*™ series and has written or co-written several of these books.

Mr. Ball previously was the co-founder and CEO of a venture capital firm that helped launch more than twenty companies including The Discovery Channel. Before that, he was a managing partner at Arthur Andersen in charge of an office that served high technology companies.

He has been an adjunct faculty member at George Mason University where he co-founded George Mason University Entrepreneurial Institute, Inc.

Mr. Ball is a certified public accountant and a member of the American Institute of Certified Public Accountants. He and his wife Dolly live in Virginia. They have two daughters, Jennifer and Stephanie.

Other books by Mr. Ball

Soar . . . If You Dare®
DNA Leadership through Goal-Driven Management
The Entrepreneur's Tool Kit
Professionalism Is for Everyone

Best Wishes for
Success and Happiness!

IF YOU WOULD LIKE more information about our other
Keep It Simple for Success titles, our discounts for
volume purchases, our speaking and leadership seminar
services, or would like to send us your comments or
suggestions, please contact or visit us at:

The Goals Institute
P.O. Box 3736
Reston, VA 20195-1736

www.goalsinstitute.com
www.kissbooks.com
Email: info@goalsinstitute.com